FOURTH OF JULY

HOLIDAYS

Lynda Sorensen

The Rourke Press, Inc.
Vero Beach, Florida 32964

Edited by Sandra A. Robinson

PHOTO CREDITS
© James P. Rowan: cover, pages 18, 21; © Lynn M. Stone: title page,
pages 12, 17; © Emil Punter/Photo Vision: page 13; courtesy National
Park Service: pages 8, 10, 15; courtesy Statue of Liberty National
Monument: page 4

Library of Congress Cataloging-in-Publication Data

Sorensen, Lynda, 1953-
    Fourth of July / Lynda Sorensen.
    p. cm. — (Holidays)
    Includes index.
    ISBN 1-57103-069-7
    1. Fourth of July—Juvenile literature. I. Title.
II. Series: Sorensen, Lynda, 1953-   Holidays.
E286.A176   1994
394.2'684—dc20   94-17724
                                                            CIP
Printed in the USA   AC

TABLE OF CONTENTS

THE FOURTH OF JULY

The Fourth of July is an American holiday that celebrates the birthday of the United States.

On July 4, 1776, a small group of Americans signed a paper called the Declaration of Independence. The Declaration of Independence said that America would no longer be ruled by England.

The first Fourth of July was the birth of America as a free and **independent** nation.

Fourth of July fireworks explode around the Statue of Liberty in New York Harbor

THE 13 COLONIES

Many settlers came to America from England in the 1600s and 1700s. The newcomers settled in several different areas. Each area had its own boundaries and was known as a **colony.**

The colonies were controlled by England. In 1776 England ruled 13 colonies in North America — Virginia, Massachusetts, New Hampshire, Maryland, Connecticut, Rhode Island, North Carolina, New York, New Jersey, Pennsylvania, Delaware, Georgia and South Carolina. Today these colonies are states, with different boundaries.

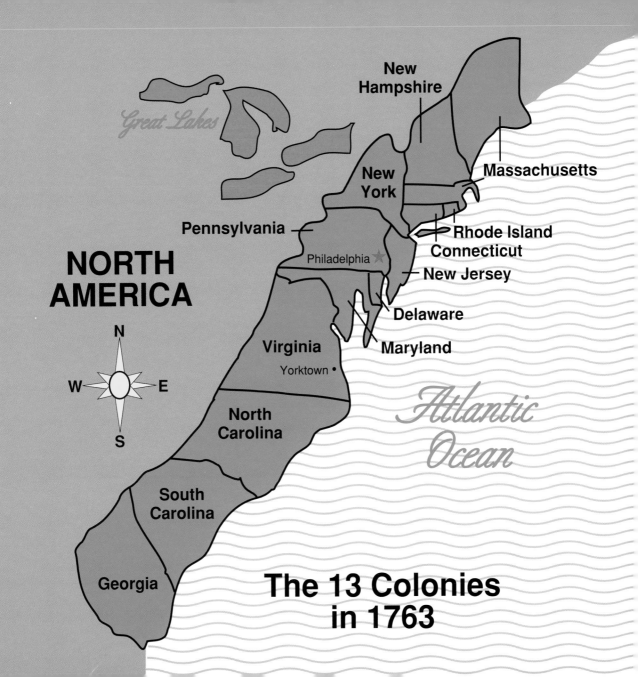

Great Lakes

New Hampshire

NORTH AMERICA

New York

Massachusetts

Pennsylvania

Philadelphia

Rhode Island
Connecticut

New Jersey

N
W E
S

Virginia

Delaware

Maryland

Yorktown •

North Carolina

Atlantic Ocean

South Carolina

Georgia

The 13 Colonies in 1763

PROBLEMS WITH KING GEORGE

In 1763, England began to force the American **colonists** to pay taxes on the things they bought from England. The colonists felt that some of the taxes were unfair. One tax, for example, made the cost of tea and paper very high.

The colonists asked the king of England, George III, to stop the taxes. King George refused.

In addition to taxes, the colonists had other problems with England.

George Washington led the American Army to victory in the war against England and King George

THE MEETING IN PHILADELPHIA

The colonies sent **delegates** to an important meeting in Philadelphia, Pennsylvania, in 1774.

The colonists held the meeting, known as the First Continental Congress, to discuss the tax laws. The delegates represented the opinions of all the people in the colonies.

The delegates voted to have the colonies stop trading goods with England until King George stopped the taxes. Still, the king refused.

The Liberty Bell in Philadelphia rang on July 8, 1776, to announce that the Continental Congress had accepted the Declaration of Independence

Many of these new American flags will be used in Fourth of July celebrations across the United States

Even "Uncle Sam" turned up at this Fourth of July parade

THE SECOND MEETING IN PHILADELPHIA

In May, 1775, delegates from the colonies met again in Philadelphia at the Second Continental Congress. By then, English soldiers and American colonists were fighting.

Total war between England and the colonies seemed likely. The delegates created a Continental Army and Navy in June, 1775. They named George Washington commander.

Independence Hall in Philadelphia was the meeting place for the Second Continental Congress and the signing of the Declaration of Independence

THE DECLARATION OF INDEPENDENCE

The colonists finally gave up hope of reaching a peaceful agreement with England. They decided that the only thing they could do was create a new nation.

The Continental Congress chose five men to explain in writing why the colonies were breaking away from England. Thomas Jefferson did most of the writing. The finished paper became the Declaration of Independence. The members of Congress approved the Declaration on July 4, 1776.

The Declaration of Independence declared that the colonies would no longer submit to English rule

WAR!

England did not want to lose its colonies. King George felt that the colonies and the goods they produced should belong to England.

England sent more soldiers to America, and battles took place throughout the colonies. Americans called this the Revolutionary War because it was a **revolution,** an effort to overthrow their government by force.

General Washington and his little army of colonists lost several battles, but they won the war. After a major defeat at Yorktown, Virginia, in 1781, England finally signed a peace treaty with the new United States on September 3, 1783.

"Weekend soldiers" — people who bring history to life — act out a Revolutionary War battle

THE FOURTH'S FIRST FIREWORKS

They were at war with England, but Americans celebrated their first year of independence on July 4, 1777, in Philadelphia. Philadelphia was the capital, or headquarters, of the Colonial Government.

American warships at Philadelphia docks fired cannons. Bells rang, bands played and fireworks exploded.

The Fourth of July has been celebrated in America every year since 1777. America had a grand 200th birthday celebration on July 4, 1976.

Americans first used fireworks to celebrate their independence on July 4, 1777

CELEBRATING THE FOURTH

The Fourth of July is a happy summer holiday for Americans. Americans wave flags, march in parades and feast at picnics. Thousands attend baseball games and other sporting events.

Fireworks are always part of Fourth of July celebrations. The bangs, booms and bright colors of fireworks help Americans say, "Happy Birthday, America!"

Glossary

colonist (KAH luh nihst) — someone who lives in a colony, especially someone who lived in England's colonies in America

colony (KAH luh nee) — a community established by a country that is beyond its own borders but still ruled by the "home" country

delegate (DEL uh guht) — a person who represents a group; a person who is elected to speak or vote for many people

independent (in deh PEN dent) — free; not controlled by others

revolution (reh vo LU shun) — people at war against their own government; a revolt